Made in United States
Troutdale, OR
11/13/2024

24736536R00056